ONE HUNDRED WAYS
TO SAY
I Love You

ONE HUNDRED WAYS
TO SAY
I Love You

COMPILED BY

Celia Haddon

Hodder & Stoughton
LONDON   SYDNEY   AUCKLAND

British Library Cataloguing in Publication Data
A record for this book is available from
the British Library

ISBN 0 346 72141 3

Printed and bound in Great Britain
by Clays Ltd. St Ives plc.

Hodder and Stoughton Ltd
A division of Hodder Headline PLC
338 Euston Road
London NW1 3BH

Contents

Declarations and Proposals

In vain have I struggled. It will not do. My feelings will not be repressed. You must allow me to tell you how ardently I admire and love you.

Mr Darcy to Elizabeth Bennett,
Pride and Prejudice,
by JANE AUSTEN,
1813

How do I love thee? Let me count the
   ways.
I love thee to the depth and breadth and
   height
My soul can reach, when feeling out of
   sight
For the ends of Being and ideal Grace.
I love thee to the level of every day's
Most quiet need, by sun and candlelight.
I love thee freely, as men strive for Right;
I love thee purely, as men turn from
   Praise.
I love thee with the passion put to use
In my old griefs, and with my
   childhood's faith.

ELIZABETH BARRETT BROWNING,
1806–61

You glow in my heart
Like the flames of uncounted candles.
But when I go to warm my hands,
My clumsiness overturns the light,
And then I stumble
Against the tables and chairs.

AMY LOWELL,
1874–1925

Pray, madam, don't put me to the expence of vows and oaths. I hate swearing under my hand. I love you in plain downright terms.

GEORGE FARQUHAR, playwright,
to Mrs C,
c. 1707

I have a cheese upon the shelf,
I cannot eat it all myself;
I have three good marks that lie in a
    rag,
In the nook the chimney instead of a
    bag:
    Say my Joan, say my Joaney, will
        that not do?
    I cannot, cannot, come every
        day to woo.

ANONYMOUS,
'The Ploughman's Wooing'

When you were a little child, as a boy I worshipped you: then when I saw you a comely girl, as a stripling I adored you: now that you are a full-grown maiden, all the rest I do, and more – I love you, more than tongue can tell, or heart can hold in silence.

John Ridd to Lorna,
Lorna Doone,
by RICHARD BLACKMORE,
1869

Come live with me, and be my love,
And we will all the pleasures prove,
That valleys, groves, and hills, and fields,
Woods or steepy mountain yields.

CHRISTOPHER MARLOWE,
1564–93

Dear, Lovely Mrs Scurlock, I have been in very good company, where your unknown name, under the character of the woman I lov'd best, has been often drunk; so that I may say I am dead drunk for your sake, which is more than 'I dye for you.'

RICHARD STEELE, essayist,
to his future wife, Mary,
1707

If 'tis love to wish you near,
To tremble when the wind I hear,
Because at sea you floating rove;
If of you to dream at night,
To languish when you're out of sight,
If this be loving, then I love.

CHARLES DIBDIN,
1745–1814

Words fail me ejaculated Bernard horsly my passion for you is intense he added fervently …When will you marry me Ethel he uttered you must be my wife it has come to that I love you so intensly that if you say no I shall perforce dash my body to the brink of yon muddy river he panted wildly.

Bernard to Ethel,
The Young Visiters,
by nine-year-old DAISY ASHFORD,
1919

I could not love thee, Dear, so much,
Lov'd I not Honour more.

SIR RICHARD LOVELACE,
1618–57

All my heart is yours, sir: it belongs to you; and with you it would remain, were fate to exile the rest of me from your presence for ever.

Jane to Mr Rochester,
Jane Eyre,
by CHARLOTTE BRONTË,
1847

i carry your heart(i carry it in my heart)

E.E. CUMMINGS,
1894–1962

Ilove you, Livy, – indeed I do love you, Livy … I love you beyond all expression, Livy – it is strange I never thought to tell you before. But I *do* love you, darling.

MARK TWAIN, writer,
to his future wife,
Olivia Langdon, 1869

Having for several Sundays had the pleasure of sitting near you in church I have been deeply impressed with a passionate love for you. My thoughts during the service are so wholly engrossed with your charms that I am afraid I require the forgiveness of heaven as well as of yourself.

The Penny Love Letter Writer:
A Complete Guide to Correspondence,
1883

Devotion and Promises

Love is my religion – I could die for that. I could die for you. My Creed is Love and you are its only tenet. You have ravish'd me away by a Power I cannot resist ...

JOHN KEATS, poet,
to Fanny Brawne,
1819

I can give not what men call love,
But wilt thou accept not
The worship the heart lifts above
And the heavens reject not ...

PERCY BYSSHE SHELLEY,
1792–1822

I t is in you that I lose myself for all
eternity, and I have no further
desires beyond this ineffable com-
munion. To thee, then, in thee and
for thee.

LÉON GAMBETTA, statesman,
to Léonie Léon,
1879

But, if thou wilt prove faithful then,
And constant of thy word,
I'll make thee glorious by my pen,
And famous by my sword ...

MARQUIS OF MONTROSE,
1612–50

There is nothing so unalterable in my heart as the intention of serving your glory; that would be glorious to me beyond all else, and I would consider it a very great victory if I could do anything that would be pleasing to you and remain acceptable to Your Grace.

Nobleman to noblewoman,
The Art of Courtly Love,
by ANDREAS CAPPELLANUS,
c. 1180

My soul can fix upon nothing but thee; thee it contemplates, admires, adores, nay depends on, trusts on you alone.

WILLIAM CONGREVE, playwright,
to Mrs Arabella Hunt,
c. 1690

As fair art thou, my bonnie lass,
  So deep in love am I,
And I will love thee still, my dear,
  Till a' the seas gang dry …

ROBERT BURNS,
1759–96

At last you are mine! Soon – in a few months, perhaps, my angel will sleep in my arms, will awaken in my arms, will live there. All your thoughts at all moments, all your looks will be for me; all my thoughts, all my moments, all my looks will be for you!

VICTOR HUGO, novelist,
to his future wife, Adèle Fouchet,
1822

My bounty is as boundless as the sea,
My love as deep; the more I give to thee,
The more I have, for both are infinite.

Juliet to Romeo, *Romeo and Juliet*,
by WILLIAM SHAKESPEARE,
1596

As I ponder and think on you, chlorides, trials, oil, Davy, steel, miscellanea, mercury, and fifty other professional fancies swim before and drive me further and further into the quandary of stupidity.

MICHAEL FARADAY, scientist,
to his future wife,
Sarah Barnard,
1820

Ye know my heart, my lady dear,
That since the time I was your thrall
I have been yours both whole and clear,
Though my reward hath been but small.
So am I yet and more than all.

THOMAS WYATT,
1503–42

I swear I will love thee with *my* whole heart and think my life well spent if it can make thine happy.

THOMAS CARLYLE, historian,
to his future wife, Jane Welsh,
1826

Earth with her flowers shall sooner
   heaven adorn;
Heaven her bright stars, through earth's
   dim globe shall move;
Fire, heat shall lose; and frosts, of
   flames be born;
Air, made to shine, as black as hell shall
   prove;
   Earth, heaven, fire, air, the world
     transformed shall view,
   Ere I prove false to faith or strange
     to you!

JOHN DOWLAND,
1563–1626

I consecrate to you my entire life, the wit I may possess, the faculties, the physical and moral forces, in exchange for this friendship so insufficient but so precious.

BENJAMIN CONSTANT, writer,
to Jeanne Récamier,
1815

Reasons for Love

Beloved, in the noisy city here,
The thought of thee can make all
   turmoil cease
Around my spirit ...

    JAMES RUSSELL LOWELL,
      1819–91

I worshipped the magnificence and the love of the God of Nature, and I thought of you; these two sensations always arise in my heart in the quiet of a rural landscape, and I have often considered it a proof of the purity and the reality of my affection for you, that it always feels most powerful in my religious moments ...

LEIGH HUNT, essayist,
to his future wife,
Marianne Kent,
1806

I love thee for thy fickleness
   And great inconstancy,
For hadst thou been a constant lass,
   Then thou hadst ne'er loved me.

ANONYMOUS,
seventeenth-century poet

I have many reasons to make me love thee whereof I will name two; first because thou lovest God, and secondly because that thou lovest me. If these were wanting, all the rest would be eclipsed.

MARGARET WINTHROP to John Winthrop, American puritan leader, 1627

I love not for those eyes, nor hair,
Nor cheeks, nor lips, nor teeth so rare,
Nor for thy speech, thy neck, nor
   breast,
Nor for thy belly, nor the rest,
Nor for thy hand nor foot so small:
But, wouldst thou know, dear sweet, for
   all.

THOMAS CAREW,
1595–1639

Thou art beautiful, O my love ...
Turn away thine eyes from me,
for they have overcome me: thy hair
is as a flock of goats that appear
from Gilead. Thy teeth are as a flock
of sheep which go up from the
washing, whereof every one beareth
twins, and there is not one barren
among them.

The Song of Solomon,
Holy Bible

Why do I love? Go, ask the glorious sun
Why every day it round the world doth
  run ...
There is no reason for our love and hate:
'Tis irresistible, as death or fate.

EPHELIA,
seventeenth century

Ask me no reason why I love you … You are not young, no more am I; go to then, there's sympathy; you are merry, so am I; ha! ha! then, there's more sympathy; you love sack and so do I; would you desire better sympathy?

Sir John Falstaff
to Mistress Anne Page,
The Merry Wives of Windsor,
by WILLIAM SHAKESPEARE,
1597

Places that are empty of you are empty of all life.

DANTE GABRIEL ROSSETTI, poet,
to Jane Morris,
1870

When thy soft accents,
    through mine ear,
Into my soul do fly,
What angel would not quit
    his sphere
To hear such harmony?

THOMAS STANLEY,
1625–78

Afore I see you, I thought all women was alike … But now … now I find what a reg'lar soft-headed, inkred'lous turnip I must ha' been; for there ain't nobody like you, though I like you better than nothin' at all . . .

Sam Weller's valentine letter
to Mary,
Pickwick Papers,
by CHARLES DICKENS,
1836

How can I see you, and not love!
While you, as opening spring, are fair?
While cold as northern blasts you prove,
How can I love! and not despair?

MATTHEW PRIOR,
1664–1721

Good God! how I feel! ... if I am not married in forty-eight hours I am no more ... I am half-dead. Good God! What will become of me? I shall go mad, most undoubtedly!

PRINCE AUGUSTUS, son of George III, to Lady Augusta Murray, 1793

Absence and the Fonder Heart

My mind, without yours, is dead
and cold as the dark midnight
river when the moon is down.

PERCY BYSSHE SHELLY
to Mary Godwin,
1814

Every moment
I'm from thy sight, the heart within my
  bosom
Moans like a tender infant in its cradle,
Whose nurse had left it.

THOMAS OTWAY,
1652–85

I weep when I reflect that you will probably not receive the first intelligence from me until Saturday – much as you love me, I love you more … Oh God! so near so far! Is our love not truly a celestial edifice – firm as Heaven's vault?

LUDWIG VAN BEETHOVEN, composer,
to an unknown woman,
1801

I sleep with thee and wake with thee,
  And yet thou art not there;
I fill my arms with thoughts of thee –
  And press the common air.
Thy eyes are gazing upon mine
  When thou art out of sight,
My lips are always touching thine
  At morning, noon, and night.

JOHN CLARE,
1793–1864

I hate this deceitful, faithless world; I think no more of it; but my wandering heart still eternally seeks you, and is filled with anguish at having lost you, in spite of all the powers of my reason.

PETER ABELARD, priest,
to Heloise, nun,
c. 1119

When I go away from you
The world beats dead
Like a slackened drum.

AMY LOWELL,
1874–1925

But how am I to live many months without seeing you? ... The hours I spend with you, I look upon as a sort of perfumed garden, a dim twilight and a fountain singing to it ... Shall I be able to endure this long exile?

GEORGE MOORE, novelist,
to Lady Cunard,
1907

I cannot be more lonely,
More drear I cannot be!
My worn heart throbs so wildly
'Twill break for thee.

EMILY BRONTË,
1818–48

I can neither eat nor sleep for thinking of you, my dearest love. I never even touch pudding.

LORD NELSON, admiral,
to Lady Hamilton,
1800

When friends are met, and goblets
  crowned,
  And smiles are near, that once
    enchanted,
Unreached by all that sunshine round,
  My soul, like some dark spot, is
    haunted
  By thee, thee, only thee.

THOMAS MOORE,
1779–1852

After I have left you, I always feel sad ... In my mind I endlessly relive your kisses, your tears, your amorous jealousy; and the many charms of peerless Josephine rage in my heart and in my senses like a scorching fire.

NAPOLEON BONAPARTE
to Josephine Bonaparte,
1796

Let's Get Physical

Give me a kiss, and to that kiss a score;
Then to that twenty, add a hundred
  more …
But yet, though love likes well such
  scenes as these,
There is an act that will more fully
  please …
Name it I would; but being blushing
  red,
The rest I'll speak, when we meet both
  in bed.

ROBERT HERRICK,
1591–1674

I would that you were in mine arms,
or I in yours – for I think it long
since I kissed you.

KING HENRY VIII
to Anne Boleyn,
1528

Roses are red, diddle diddle, violets are
   blue,
If you'll have me, diddle diddle, I will
   have you.

WOMEN'S LEAP-YEAR
TRADITIONAL BALLAD

Would that thou werest only now
by my side. There are
everywhere large wide beds and thou
shouldst have no cause to complain ...

JOHANN WOLFGANG VON GOETHE,
   writer, to Christiane Vulpius,
               1792

O my bonny, bonny May,
    Will ye not rue upon me;
A sound, sound sleep I'll never get,
    Until I lye ayont thee.

SCOTTISH POPULAR SONG,
1776

I am maddened by a longing to seize you in my arms and kiss you. Were you here, I'd bite you: that is what I want to do. Women once reproached me for being cold . . . Yet deep within me now lurks the appetite of a wild beast, and the sex instinct of a love carnivore longing to tear you to pieces . . .

GUSTAVE FLAUBERT, novelist,
to Louise Colet,
1846

I have seen only you, I have admired only you, I desire only you.

EMPEROR NAPOLEON BONAPARTE,
note to Marie Walewska,
1807

At your approach my heart beats fast
  within me;
A pleasing trembling thrills thro' all my
  blood,
Whene'er you touch me with your
  melting hand:
But when you kiss, oh! 'tis not to be
  spoke!

> ANONYMOUS,
> date unknown

Some people like sex more than others –
You seem to like it a lot.
There's nothing wrong with being
  innocent or high-minded
But I'm glad you're not.

      WENDY COPE,
        living poet

I dreamt of you all night, and in spite of your rigour I had you in my arms, it is impossible to describe the ecstacy, 'twould be too transporting to be revealed . . .

GEORGE FARQUHAR, playwright,
to Mrs C,
c. 1701.

I know your lust
Is love.

EDWARD THOMAS,
1878–1917

Make me thy maiden chamber-man,
Or let me be thy warming-pan.

ANONYMOUS,
seventeenth century

Accusations, Apologies and Denials

I know I do not love thee! yet, alas!
Others will scarcely trust my candid
    heart;
And oft I catch them smiling as they
    pass,
Because they see me gazing where thou
    art.

CAROLINE NORTON,
1808–77

I take my pen again to tell you that I am at your knees, that I still love you, that I detest you sometimes, that the day before yesterday I said horrible things about you, that I kiss your beautiful hands, that I kiss them again pending something better, that I am at the end of my tether, that you are divine, etc.

ALEXANDER PUSHKIN, writer,
to Anna Petrovna Kern,
1825

When I read in your looks and words that you love me, I feel it in the deepest part of my soul; then I care not one straw for the whole Universe beside; but when you fly from my caresses to – smoke tobacco, or speak of me as a new *circumstance* of your lot, then in deed my 'heart is troubled about many things'.

JANE WELSH,
to her future husband,
Thomas Carlyle, historian,
1826

But if my constant love shall fail to
   move thee,
Then know my reason hates thee,
   though I love thee.

THOMAS CAREW,
1595–1639

You pierce my soul. I am half agony, half hope … I have loved none but you. Unjust I may have been, weak and resentful I have been, but never inconstant.

Captain Frederick Wentworth
to Anne Elliot,
Persuasion,
by JANE AUSTEN,
1818

Thus, whether we're on or we're off,
Some witchery seems to await you;
To love you is pleasant enough,
But oh! 'tis delicious to hate you!

THOMAS MOORE
1779-1852

I do not love you at all: on the contrary I detest you. You are an uncouth creature, stupid and good for nothing …Soon I hope to take you in my arms and cover you with a million burning kisses, as hot as the equator.

NAPOLEON BONAPARTE,
to his wife Josephine,
1796.

My love is as a fever, longing still
For that which longer nurseth the
   disease ...
   For I have sworn thee fair and
     thought thee bright
Who art as black as hell, as dark
   as night.

WILLIAM SHAKESPEARE,
1564–1616

May I presume to beg pardon ...
You shall see me prostrate
before you and use me like a slave
while I kiss the dear feet that trample
upon me.

WILLIAM CONGREVE, playwright,
to Mrs Arabella Hunt,
c. 1690

My dear, why make you more of a dog
   than me?
  If he do love, I burn, I burn in love:
  If he wait well, I never thence would
    move:
If he be fair, yet but a dog can be.

SIR PHILIP SIDNEY,
1554–86

What a dishclout of a soul hast thou made of me? ... Does it add to your triumph, that your eyes and lips have turned a man into a fool, whom the rest of the town is courting as a wit?

> LAURENCE STERNE, novelist,
> to Lady Percy,
> 1765

You do bewitch me! O that I could fly
From my self you, or from your own
    self I!

> MICHAEL DRAYTON,
> 1563–1631

I do not love thee,
Yet joy's very essence
Comes with thy footstep
Is complete in thy presence.

JOHN CLARE,
1793–1864

Wives and Husbands

I am so entirely yours, that if I might have all the world given me, I could not be happy but in your love.

DUKE OF MARLBOROUGH, general, to his wife Sarah, 1703.

You will not believe what a longing for you possesses me ... I lie awake a great part of the night thinking of you ...

PLINY THE YOUNGER,
to his wife, Calpurnia,
first century AD

I look back, and in every one point, every word and gesture, *every* letter, every silence – you have been entirely perfect to me – I would not change one word, one look. My hope and aim are to preserve this love, not to fall from it ...

ROBERT BROWNING, poet,
to Elizabeth Barrett, on the day
of their secret marriage,
1846

This to the crown and blessing of my
  life,
The much loved husband of a happy
  wife;
To him whose constant passion found
  the art
To win a stubborn and ungrateful heart;
And to the world by tenderest proof
  discovers
They err, who say that husbands can't
  be lovers.

ANNE FINCH,
Countess of Winchilsea
1661–1720

I have nothing to tell you, except that I love you, which, I fear, you will think rather dull.

BENJAMIN DISRAELI, statesman,
to his wife Mary Ann,
note sent by a footman,
1872

On my last great disappointment I should have lost my courage *but for you* – my little darling wife. You are my *greatest* and *only* stimulus now, to battle with this uncongenial, unsatisfactory, and ungrateful life.

EDGAR ALLAN POE, writer,
to his wife Virginia,
1846

Every sentence should claim you, as my own dear wife, the pride of my youth, the joy of my manhood, the hope of all my after days.

THOMAS HOOD, poet,
to his wife Jane,
1835

I am fast shut up like a little lake in the embrace of some big mountains, you would see me down below, deep and shining – and quite fathomless, my dear. You might drop your heart into me and you'd never hear it touch bottom.

KATHERINE MANSFIELD, writer,
to her husband,
John Middleton Murry,
1918

I could not live if I lost you. I do not think one could conceive of a love more exclusive, more tender, or more pure than I have for you. I think it is immortal, a thing which happens seldom.

VITA SACKVILLE-WEST, gardener, to her husband, Harold Nicolson, 1929

If ever two were one, then surely we.
If ever man were loved by wife, then
thee.
If ever wife was happy in a man,
Compare with me, ye woman, if you
can.
I prize thy love more than whole mines
of gold,
Or all the riches that the east doth hold.

ANNE BRADSTREET,
1612–72

Dear Prue, – I am very sleepy and tired, but could not think of closing my eyes till I had told you I am, dearest creature, your most affectionate and faithful husband.

RICHARD STEELE, to his wife,
1710

You are a Poem. Of what sort, then? Epic? Mercy on me, no! A sonnet? No, for that is too labored and artificial. You are a sort of sweet, simple, gay pathetic ballad ...

NATHANIEL HAWTHORNE, writer,
to his wife Sophia,
1839

Endings and Farewells

Stay, O sweet, and do not rise,
The light that shines comes from thine
    eyes;
The day breaks not, it is my heart,
Because that you and I must part.

JOHN DONNE,
1572-1631

Ten thousand times farewell – yet stay a
  while.
Sweet, kiss me once: sweet kisses time
  beguile.

> ROBERT JONES,
> seventeenth century

The morn hath not the glory that it
  wore,
Nor doth the day so beautifully die,
Since I can call thee to my side no
  more,
To gaze upon the sky.

> WILLIAM CULLEN BRYANT,
> to his dead wife,
> 1794–1878

May you not rest as long as I am living! ... Be with me always – take any form – drive me mad! only *do* not leave me in this abyss, where I cannot find you!

Heathcliff
to the dead Catherine Earnshaw,
Wuthering Heights,
by EMILY BRONTË,
1847

Shake hands, we shall never be friends,
    all's over;
        I only vex you the more I try.
All's wrong that ever I've done or said,
And nought to help it in this dull head;
        Shake hands, here's luck, goodbye.

But if you come to a road where
    danger
        Or guilt of anguish or shame's to
        share,
Be good to the lad that loves you true
And the soul that was born to die for
    you,
        And whistle and I'll be there.

ALFRED EDWARD HOUSMAN,
1859–1936

To My Widow …I take advantage of a very small measure of warmth to write letters preparatory to a possible end – the first is naturally to you on whom my thoughts mostly dwell waking or sleeping. If anything happens to me I should like you to know how much you have meant to me, what pleasant recollections are with me as I depart.

ROBERT FALCON SCOTT's last letter
from the Antarctic
to his wife Kathleen,
1912

Eyes, look your last!
Arms, take your last embrace! and lips,
  O you
The doors of breath, seal with a
  righteous kiss,
A dateless bargain to engrossing death.

Romeo to Juliet,
Romeo and Juliet,
by WILLIAM SHAKESPEARE,
1596

Most noble Christian queen, I beseech you, as ye have been ever my special good lady, and I your true and poor knight unto my power, and as I never failed you in right nor yet in wrong, that ye will pray for my soul if that I be slain.

Sir Lancelot to Queen Guenevere,
Le Morte D'Arthur ,
by SIR THOMAS MALORY,
c. 1470

Mine eyes wax heavy and ye day grows
   old.
The dew falls thick, my belov'd grows
   cold.
Draw, draw ye closed curtains: and
   make room:
My dear, my dearest dust: I come, I
   come.

LADY CATHERINE DYER,
seventeenth century

All the beautiful time is yours for always, for it is life that takes away, changes and spoils so often – not death, which is really the warden and not the thief of our treasures.

'In Memoriam' column,
The Times,
1931

Acknowledgments

There are some copyrights in this book which I could not trace. The publishers will be happy to rectify any omissions in future editions. I would like to thank the following:

The Society of Authors for an extract from *Letters of Katherine Mansfield to John Middleton Murry*, and for 'Shake hands, we shall never be friends, all's over', in *More Poems XXX*, by A. E. Housman.

Columbia University Press for an extract from *The Art of Courtly Love*, by Andreas Cappellanus, edited by John Jay Parry © 1941 Columbia University Press. Reprinted with the permission of the publisher.

Faber and Faber for a verse, 'From June to December V Some People', from *Making Cocoa for Kingsley Amis*, by Wendy Cope. Reprinted with permission of Faber and Faber.

HarperCollins Publishers Ltd for an extract from *H. Nicolson, Diaries and Letters*, edited by Nigel Nicolson, 1930–1939, vol. 1, Wm Collins.

W.W. Norton & Company for permission to quote from 'i carry your heart with me(i carry it in' which is reprinted from *Complete Poems 1904–1962*,

by E.E. Cummings, edited by George J. Firmage,
by permission of W.W. Norton & Company.
Copyright © 1991 by the Trustees for the E.E.
Cummings Trust and George James Firmage.

Random House for an extract from *The Young Visiters*
by Daisy Ashford, Chatto and Windus.

Oxford University Press for an extract from *The Letters
of John Keats*, edited by M. Buxton Forman, Oxford
University Press, 1952, and an extract from *Dante
Gabriel Rossetti and Jane Morris; Their Correspondence*,
edited by John Bryson with Janet Camp Troxell,
Clarendon Press, 1976. Reprinted by permission of
Oxford University Press.

Colin Smythe Ltd on behalf of the heirs of the Estate
of C.D. Medley for an extract from *George Moore –
Letters to Lady Cunard*, edited by C.D. Medley,
Rupert Hart Davies, 1957.

J. Thomas Shaw for his translation of the portion of a
Pushkin letter to Anna Petrovna Kern, from his
book, *The Letters of Alexander Pushkin*, translated,
edited and with an Introduction by J. Thomas
Shaw, 3 vols., Philadelphia: Univ. of Pennsylvania
Press, and Bloomington: Indiana Univ. Press,
1963.

University of California Press for an extract from *Mark
Twain's Letters*, vol. 3, 1869, edited and translated
by Victor Fischer. Copyright ©1992 The Mark
Twain Foundation.

Also compiled by Celia Haddon

ONE HUNDRED WAYS

TO
Serenity

Find quiet moments in a busy day to dip into
these quotations on peace and serenity and you
will find support and inspiration from common
proverbs to great authors.

If the bell rings, why should we run?
Time is just a stream I go a fishing in.
HENRY DAVID THOREAU

I am an old man and have had many troubles,
but most of them never happened.
VICTORIAN INSCRIPTION

Be not disturbed at trifles, or at
accidents common or unavoidable.
BENJAMIN FRANKLIN

Conquer by accepting.
BISHOP HILLMAN STREETER

Hodder & Stoughton
0 340 71417 4